DEBT P
EXP

GW00832587

The Bankr....
Guide to Serious Debt Problems

DEBT PROBLEMS EXPLAINED

The Bankruptcy Association's
Guide to Serious Debt Problems

John McQueen
and
Gill Hankey

The Bankruptcy Association
of Great Britain and Ireland

THIS BOOK IS A PUBLICATION OF

The Bankruptcy Association
of Great Britain and Ireland

4 Johnson Close
Abraham Heights
Lancaster
Lancashire
LA1 5EU
United Kingdom
Tel: (01524) 64305

ISBN 0 9518636 1 4

Typeset and Printed by Redwood Books

Contents

The Bankruptcy Association's motto:

If you lived in the richest, most powerful city it was possible for a man to imagine, but there was no love there, no mercy and no justice for those who met with misfortune; then you would be better off dead than to live in such a place.

****

Authors' dedications:

For those people past who live on in my heart: My Mum and Dad as always; my lovely brothers, James and William; my little sister, Nancy and my much missed nephew, Damian.

John McQueen

****

For the two most important people in my life – my husband, Ted and my daughter, Joanne. Together, we are unbeatable!

Gill Hankey

****

FOREWORD

Between us, the two authors of this book have more than 20 years experience advising people in serious debt. Together, day in and day out, we run the Bankruptcy Association which is an independent national organisation that offers personal advice to people in debt.

Few books are written by authors who are just a telephone call away from their readers. It is this personal touch that has been greatly appreciated by the tens of thousands of people who have sought our advice over many years.

There are currently more than three thousand people who are subscribing members of the Bankruptcy Association. These people, coming from every walk of life imaginable, provided us with the inspiration to write this book. We deal with people with serious debt problems every working day of our lives. We advise them, we cajole them, we sympathise with them and, sometimes, we even have to give them some hard home truths.

We are here every working day, each in our own office in our own homes, carrying out the work that has taken over both our lives. We have heard – many times – grown men and women crying down the telephone gripped in the depths of the despair that debt can bring. This despair can become so deep that each year many people take the ultimate step of committing suicide as a result.

We also know, from personal experience, the pain of being in debt. We have both personally experienced loss of homes, businesses, family breakdowns and all the other traumas associated with debt problems. We understand why people sometimes cry. We have cried too.

Money rules our society. There is no escape from this unless someone is prepared to live as a tramp or a hermit and even those characters will need some money, sometime. We all need – one way or another – some of the filthy lucre in order to simply survive. This is why people on low wages are forced to borrow money in order to buy essentials and why others, in an attempt to create work and an income for themselves, risk their all in business ventures.

The consequences are as inevitable as car accidents. Tens of thousands of people find themselves crushed down with unbearable debts each year when urgent action is required. This book is designed to help such people focus on potential solutions to their problems. It is based on the tried and tested common-sense procedures that we have used in advising people over many years.

Previously published Bankruptcy Association books, and other current Bankruptcy Association books, have been and are being, very well received by their many thousands of readers. We hope that this book will be as well received as our others.

This book is based on the law as it stands in England and Wales on 1 July 1997. Scotland has some distinctive legal features which are not covered in this book. The general guidance, however, is as applicable in Scotland as elsewhere in the United Kingdom.

John McQueen	Gill Hankey
Lancaster	Kingston upon Hull
27 August 1997	27 August 1997

CHAPTER 1

FACING THE FACTS

Based on our long experience running the Bankruptcy Association, it would appear that about one person in every ten is absolutely on the ball regarding their personal finances. Such people will know, down to the last penny, the exact balance in their bank account and will operate immaculate weekly or monthly budgets. Such people will rarely find themselves with debt problems they cannot handle because they are likely to be extremely cautious in all aspects of their financial affairs.

At the other end of the scale, about one person in every ten is utterly hopeless with money. They cannot budget, indeed they have probably never heard of the word and spend their lives hopelessly in debt, moving from one financial crisis to the next. We feel sure that every reader will recognize these characteristics in someone within their own family or social circle.

The majority of people, the other eight out of ten, fall in between these two extremes. They will be reasonably financially competent at heart, but prone to making financial mistakes at times, as the problems in life take their toll. Sometimes life events will bring problems. Divorce, for example, is a major cause of debt problems because of the financial stresses and burdens it often brings. Many students also leave university these days, saddled with large loans they have had to borrow to get through university. Anyone going into business takes a major gamble with their personal finances.

1

Personal habits can also cause financial problems. For example, smoking and drinking are expensive financial pastimes. Also, many people in Britain are paid very low wages or they are dependent entirely upon State benefits.

For various reasons therefore, millions of basically honest and decent British people find themselves saddled with serious debt problems. This book is aimed at people with serious debts and at business people who run into financial trouble. The book is also designed to demystify debt issues. Many debt advice books, in our opinion, simply confuse people with too much detailed discussion of unimportant side issues.

The method we have adopted is a simple head-on approach. We take the view that someone in debt has four basic choices. They can pay their debts in full, pay them in part, go bankrupt or run away. It is as simple as that. In the following chapter we discuss these issues in more detail as they appertain to the ordinary consumer debtor. Chapter 3 discusses these issues as they relate to people running businesses. Chapter 5 looks at how those people running limited companies should deal with financial problems.

People have different personalities and attitudes towards money. In addition, people bring their own emotional baggage with them into their particular financial position. Every individual has their own internalised feelings and prejudices. No book can deal adequately with these vastly complicated differences between people. Some people in debt are more laconic and laid back about financial matters than others, for instance.

Money itself, however, has no personality. This is the key point and it applies to all people in debt. It is a much sought after commodity. Creditors get upset and angry if people who owe them money do not pay them. They will retaliate by taking various actions to try and recover that money. This is when the distress starts, with bailiffs and

2

other collectors knocking on doors trying to recover money owed. This is a brutal process that takes no account of individual sensitivities. Well educated, highly competent people can be made to feel extremely humiliated by the legal processes involved in recovering money.

The important concept we wish to get over to readers therefore, is the paramount need to face the financial facts in as cool and dispassionate a manner as possible. Try to avoid feeling shame or humiliation if in debt. Money is just number crunching. The numbers decide the action that must be taken. We hope this book will enable readers in debt to very quickly see the important line of action they need to take.

We very deliberately do not go into fine details because, as we have argued above, fine details can cloud worried minds. Worried people in debt often cannot cope with such detail. The important point for such people is that they recognize the basic avenue to follow, and then travel down it.

CHAPTER 2

THE CONSUMER DEBTOR

By the term 'consumer debtor' we mean anyone in debt who is not running a business and who typically has run up a serious debt or debts. Literally millions of people fall into this category. They face problems such as mortgage and rent arrears, rates arrears, credit card debts, bank loans, student loans, and a vast variety of other debts it is possible for an individual to accrue in our society.

It is very easy to fall into serious debt, but much more difficult to climb out of it. That is the lesson we have drawn from the thousands of individuals in debt we have advised in our work for the Bankruptcy Association.

There are, of course, a few high earning individuals around who fall into debt difficulties but then manage to earn their way out of trouble. The majority of debtors, however, find the trail back to solvency very difficult indeed.

What makes an Individual Insolvent?

Before going further we need to consider when it is that an individual can be considered to be insolvent. Fortunately this can be easily explained and needs to be understood by anyone with financial problems. An individual is insolvent when he cannot meet his financial commitments on the dates they become due.

This definition, of course, would classify most of us, at one time or another, as insolvent. Fail to pay that electricity or rates bill on time and you are technically insolvent. Even

4

the most carefully run households will find themselves in that position from time to time – perhaps because some emergency has arisen.

The description of an individual as solvent or insolvent is often – wrongly – associated with debt/assets ratios. People with assets worth far more than their debts can be and are made bankrupt because they cannot pay their debts on the date due. This has happened to many people in recent years due to the collapse of the property market and lack of job security. For example, take a couple, both in employment, who own a house worth around £50,000, with a mortgage of £30,000. They both lose their jobs and are unable to pay their credit cards bills and eventually arrears build up on their mortgage account. Although they place their property on the market for sale, they are unable to locate a purchaser. Eventually their building society seeks possession of their home and they come under increasing pressure from credit card companies. Their only income is State benefit and their debts increase virtually daily. Their home is then sold by the building society for less than the mortgage outstanding and not only do they have their credit card debts, but they are faced with a mortgage shortfall. Within a very short period of time they have gone from being in employment, with their own home to a potential bankruptcy situation.

So the threat of insolvency is ever present to most individuals, and our credit orientated society is now pushing more and more individuals over the often narrow line which separates solvent from insolvent individuals.

The Key Concepts

The key concepts then, are that an individual is insolvent when he cannot meet his financial commitments when they fall due, and he becomes solvent again when he can, by whatever method, meet his future financial commitments on time. This is the only sensible financial barometer that matters from the point of view of an individual debtor.

The goalposts for any particular individual are therefore very clearly defined. However, just as in a football match the methods of reaching the goal can be infinitely varied. Sometimes there will be a quick and easy solution – such as selling a high priced home, moving down market and clearing off a chain of debts at a stroke. On other occasions a lot of tortuous dribbling will have to take place. This is because some individuals will have no easy options and may have to enter into complex negotiations with many creditors.

In other words, the methods of returning an individual to solvency can be infinitely varied and there is ample scope for creative thinking and action here by individual debtors. That said, each individual in debt is faced with four basic choices: These are:

1) REPAY DEBTS IN FULL
2) REPAY DEBTS IN PART
3) GO BANKRUPT
4) RUN AWAY

REPAY DEBTS IN FULL
Budgeting

By definition, it will follow that the budgets (although they may not formally exist), of all insolvent individuals are out of balance. The starting point for a debtor is therefore to draw up a weekly or monthly budget. A strict analysis needs to be carried out of all income and expenditure. If, on examination, the financial commitments of an individual cannot be met from the budget, then at least one of the following needs to be considered:

1) Increase income (perhaps through overtime or a part-time job, or by checking that all appropriate

government allowances are being claimed).
2) Reduce all unnecessary expenditure (is that rented video recorder really necessary?).
3) Contact all creditors, making them aware of the current difficulties. Open negotiations with those creditors to reduce payments in line with the funds available.Although most creditors will accept reduced payments, at least for a short period of time to allow the debtor 'breathing space' to perhaps increase his/her income, restructure his finances, etc. most will expect the interest to be paid and more than likely a token sum paid off the capital.
4) Pay creditors in priority order: ie mortgage payments or rent, rates, electricity, water and gas have priority over credit card debts, TV rental etc.

By the implementation of a simple budget very many people will quickly find their own solutions.

Assistance from Friends and Family

Some people may be fortunate enough to have friends and relatives willing to help them to solve their debt problems. A gift or an interest free loan may provide a solution to debt problems. However, we would stress the need for caution if any reader is contemplating this action as we have come across many people who have accepted gifts of money from relatives. These funds have then only partially solved their debt problems and they have ended up in bankruptcy anyway. In these cases the funds provided by relatives have simply been wasted. It is important for anyone borrowing funds or indeed accepting a gift of money to supposedly help them, that they view their current problems realistically. Many people fail to face up to the magnitude of their financial position and live with the hope that they are able to put the matter right, when there is little realistic possibility of doing so. It is very distressing and worrying to cope with debts, but it is even worse if funds from friends and family are also lost in a failed attempt to resolve the original problem. These points should be kept in mind by anyone seeking financial assistance from friends or relatives.

Refinancing

Although the old adage "never borrow from Peter to pay Paul" may have made sense in the context of our grandparents and parents way of life, it is definitely not true in a social context of widespread property ownership.

Very often it makes perfectly good sense to replace one type of debt with another. For instance, it makes perfect sense to replace a string of credit card debts on high rates of interest with a secured second mortgage on a much lower rate of interest and therefore a smaller monthly repayment. Readers, however, need to be aware that there are rogue loan sharks about who offer second mortgages at crippling rates of interest and who also charge fees for arranging that second mortgage. These should be avoided like the plague. Only deal with reputable, well known companies and never agree to pay arrangement fees.

Social attitudes can often be amusing. One lady who we advised a short time ago to take that course of action said "Oh, but if I take out a second mortgage – I will be in debt then! " She took some convincing that she was in debt whatever form that debt took. The risk of losing one's home is just as great (and possibly greater) from an unsecured creditor if they bring a bankruptcy petition, as it is from possession proceedings resulting from first or second mortgage default. The point is that any form of debt can result in a home being lost. Many individuals have been put back on a solvent footing by sensible restructuring of their debts.

Some individuals, however, will find themselves in such

serious difficulties that the possible solutions outlined above will just not work and more drastic action will be required. If court orders are flying about and an individual appears to be hopelessly insolvent then a drastic legal remedy may be called for. The following should be considered:

Negotiate with Creditors

Sensible negotiations with creditors are very often the best possible way of dealing with many debt problems. Most creditors (although not all) are reasonable people and will adopt a more sympathetic line if they are made aware of the problem and offered some sensible proposals. They will very often, if the personal circumstances merit it, be prepared to extend the period that was originally agreed for repayment. If a proper explanation is provided and details of income and expenditure made available, then most creditors will be accommodating about allowing extra time to pay.

REPAY DEBTS IN PART
Negotiate with Creditors

If the debts of a particular individual are so high that there is no reasonable prospect of repaying them over a reasonable time, then it may be possible to negotiate with creditors for them to accept a proportion of the debt in full and final settlement. Creditors normally expect to be repaid in full. That is the basis on which money is lent and money is borrowed. If, however, it is made clear to creditors that if they do not agree to accept a proportion of their debt in full and final settlement, then the only alternative will be for the borrower to go into bankruptcy, thereby giving them a nil return on their debt, then most creditors will give serious consideration to such an offer. If a creditor is to accept a proportion of the debt in full and final settlement, then that creditor will no doubt expect the agreed amount by way of a lump sum payment. For example, a creditor may be prepared to accept a single payment of £500 to settle a £2,000 debt. They would be most unlikely, however, to accept an offer of £50 a month paid over 10 months.

People in debt often cannot understand why creditors are usually unwilling to accept such repayments in instalments. There is, however, an easy explanation. Creditors know from long experience that instalment deals more often than not break down and do not last the course. In addition they have the extra administrative costs to bear at the same time as being asked to accept a proportion of the debt in full and final settlement. It is also important to understand when trying to negotiate along the above lines that creditors will have to be satisfied that the debtor is willing to give up any available assets. For example, if someone owed £10,000 and that person owned a home with £5000 of equity available if it were to be sold, then the creditor would expect at least this amount of money to be made available to them. Creditors will only be prepared to accept a proportion of their debt in full and final settlement if the debtor has no disposable income and no assets. A debtor cannot expect a creditor to accept a loss and leave him, the debtor with assets and/or disposable income.

Administration Orders

Individuals who have at least one judgement debt outstanding against them can apply to their local county court for an administration order, if their total debts are below £5,000. If an administration order is granted then all the debts are brought under a single umbrella and the debtor makes a single regular payment as agreed, to the court which then distributes it, on a pro-rata basis to creditors.

There are, however, some major (and surprising) local differences in how they work. In some areas the court will treat a mortgage debt as part of the global debts of an individual, thus excluding many individuals from the protection of an administration order. In other areas mortgage debts are simply not taken into account. In a few areas, too, it is possible to offer a creditor a dividend of say 25p in the £ in full and final settlement, rather than full repayment. In other areas full repayment is expected, with statutory interest. Therefore it is important to check on the local rules.

Administration orders can be an extremely effective way to return an individual to solvency in appropriate cases. Applications can be made by individuals directly to the court. However, the forms may seem complex to some people and many Citizens Advice Bureaux have debt counsellors who will assist people to complete these. Alternatively it may be possible to call upon the services of a member of family or a friend who is more familiar with paperwork.

Individual Voluntary Arrangement

It is now possible for individual debtors to enter into a formal voluntary arrangement known as an IVA (individual voluntary arrangement). These arrangements are legal contracts for the satisfaction of debts, either in whole or in part, and such arrangements, if voted in, are binding on all unsecured creditors, subject to limited technical exceptions which may cause difficulties.

We were very keen on these arrangements when they first became available in 1987 and encouraged hundreds of people to take this route. However, bitter experience of watching them fail, time after time, often because of excessive demands made by creditors, and inadequate or incorrect advice given by so-called professional advisers, have left us very wary of recommending this course of action.

A voluntary arrangement is an offer made to unsecured creditors, by an individual in financial trouble, to perhaps dispose of assets and/or make a contribution from future earnings, to pay out a dividend to those unsecured creditors in full settlement of their debts. Secured creditors may also be bound by the arrangement as long as they have been given notice of their entitlement to vote. A proposal must be made to, and through, an insolvency practitioner, who is a person specifically authorised to deal with such matters. Insolvency practitioners are usually qualified as either accountants or solicitors. In practice, they help prepare the proposal and should act as an independent intermediary between the debtor and the creditors, thereby ensuring that the proposal is realistic and represents a fair balance between the interests of all concerned. Once a proposal has been prepared, an application is made to the court for an Interim Order. This protects the debtor from further legal action by creditors. That protection prevents the issue of a bankruptcy petition or the hearing of a petition which has already been issued. The purpose is to maintain the current position until the creditors have had the opportunity to consider the proposal, at a meeting called by the insolvency practitioner for that purpose. Such a meeting will be called, unless the insolvency practitioner reports to the court that there is no reasonable prospect of reaching an agreement with the creditors.

Arrangements may involve the disposal of assets, so that the proceeds may be shared amongst the creditors. Payments may be made by the debtor from future income or from trading receipts. Sometimes funds may be made available by a friend or relative, in return for creditors accepting the proposal. Any combination is possible. Often the debtor will wish to keep his home, in return for payments from his future earnings or from a third party.

All creditors may vote on the proposal, either by being

present in person, by sending a representative or by sending a postal vote. The votes of secured creditors only count to the extent that their security is insufficient to cover their lending. Voting power is according to money owed to individual creditors. It then requires the agreement of 75 per cent, by money value, of those creditors who trouble to vote, and whose votes are valid, to turn the proposal into a binding voluntary arrangement. This is subject to the proviso that there are at least 50 per cent in favour, ignoring the votes of connected persons, ie 'close relatives.'

If a voluntary arrangement succeeds, then bankruptcy is avoided. In law, individuals may then incur further credit. In reality, this is often found to be impossible as their credit rating is ruined because voluntary arrangements are recorded by credit reference agencies.

The costs of setting up the voluntary arrangement and supervising the implementation of it, if approved, should come from the monies which the arrangement provides to be distributed to creditors. In reality, however, most insolvency practitioners will be unwilling to act unless some, if not all, of the initial costs are paid to them in advance. This is because, if the arrangement is not approved, there will be no funds to cover their fees. Depending on the complexity of the case and the area in which the debtor resides, these costs can range between £1,000 and £5,000.

Anyone entering into a voluntary arrangement must adhere strictly to the agreed terms, otherwise the insolvency practitioner supervising the arrangement has little choice but to apply for the bankruptcy of the person involved. A good arrangement should allow some flexibility in the event of unforeseen circumstances. When arrangements do fail mid-term, the misery of the debt problem has simply been extended and because there are bankruptcy costs as well as the costs of the arrangement which went before, creditors also suffer a detriment.

It should also be pointed out that even if a bankruptcy order has been made against an individual, then a voluntary arrangement may still be attempted. If successful, it will have the effect of lifting the bankruptcy order.

There are many sharks in the insolvency world, some advertise in national newspapers, claiming to be able to save people from bankruptcy. These sharks often simply refer people to insolvency practitioners, collecting a fat fee for themselves, en route. From their own selfish point of view, it is in their interest to encourage people to go for voluntary arrangements, when this may not be the best option for the debtor. Those who are in financial difficulty should ensure that they contact someone appropriately experienced to give them guidance, such as the Bankruptcy Association.

To sum up, individual voluntary arrangements should be approached with extreme caution and they should only be considered if there is some real, practical benefit to the person involved. The mere avoidance of bankruptcy itself is not, in our view, sufficient justification for entering into such an arrangement.

This procedure is available to people resident in Northern Ireland as well as England and Wales, but is not available in Scotland.

GO BANKRUPT

If it is not possible to reach an agreement with creditors and the burden of debt therefore continues, then any debtor has the option of going bankrupt. Readers should now turn to chapter 4 to consider the full implications of taking this avenue.

RUN AWAY

A few people simply decide to run away from their money problems. This may be in a physical sense, ie they may move house, leaving no forwarding address or perhaps flee abroad. They may run away in a mental sense by simply ignoring all approaches/action by creditors. In our wide experience these are very foolish avenues to take indeed. The person who runs away is often constantly worrying about being caught up with and can only live life in a constant state of trepidation. There are a few thick-skinned individuals who can perhaps live with such behaviour, but even these people are foolish for another, very important, reason.

A person who runs away from his creditors can be bankrupted in his absence. Any creditor owed £750 or more can apply to have a debtor bankrupted. If someone who runs away is bankrupted then that person may well be held in bankruptcy until such time as they reappear. This means that if the person who runs away subsequently rebuilds his life and perhaps buys property, then all this will be lost if, or when, they are discovered later. We have known several people to whom this has happened.

In other words, for a person to adopt this cause of action means that that person must spend the rest of his life with a 'Sword of Damocles' hanging over his head. If a person is under such financial pressure that he feels like running away then it makes much more sense to at least go bankrupt first because he will then be discharged from the bankruptcy after a few years and be able to breathe easily again. If, therefore, any reader is considering running away, we strongly advise against it for the reasons given above.

OTHER IMPORTANT ISSUES

The above summarises the options available to a person in serious debt. Some people, however, have various other complications to deal with, as well as having to decide how to deal with their problem. It is not the intention of this book to go into all the complex legal side issues. We do, however, discuss briefly below, laid out in alphabetical order, some of the more common side issues we are often requested to comment upon:

Ambulance Chasers

There are a wide variety of commercial so-called 'debt advisers.' Some of these are properly licensed, many are not. They tout for business by writing to people who are in receipt of court judgements or bankruptcy petitions and by putting alluring advertisements in newspapers offering to get debts written off. In many cases they simply cannot achieve what they offer and most of these people should be strenuously avoided. Some are just looking to collect a fee and then do nothing, others are simply 'fronts' for insolvency practitioners trying to ensnare people into entering into the individual voluntary arrangements described above. This is usually an expensive, unnecessary and unworkable procedure. We deal with individuals on a daily basis who have, to put it bluntly, been 'ripped off', often for many hundreds if not thousands of pounds, with no benefit to them whatsoever.

Attachment of Earnings

County courts and Magistrates courts can make orders instructing employers to deduct payments directly from employees wages. This can be done when someone has defaulted on an Order of the court to make a regular payment to a creditor or has failed to pay an instalment of a fine.

Bailiffs

Bailiffs are people who act on behalf of creditors, or the courts, to collect debts, seize goods or to repossess homes. There are many types of bailiffs all with varying powers. Many people ask us each year about the rights and powers of bailiffs. Their powers vary according to the debt they are attempting to collect and, without a textbook on the complexities of bailiffs powers imprinted in our minds, it is generally impossible to say. In any event, many bailiffs themselves are unaware of their precise powers. Common sense needs to be applied when someone turns up on the doorstep with a court order claiming to be a bailiff.

If bailiffs arrive to repossess a home they have the power to physically remove people from a repossessed home and seize the property. If they arrive to collect unpaid debts they generally have the power to seize goods belonging to the debtor. In most cases they cannot seize personal belongings, bedding or items of household furniture necessary for everyday living. If they try to seize such intimate possessions they should be physically prevented until confirmation of the terms of any court order is precisely investigated and confirmed. They can often also take 'walking possession' of goods. This means that they make a list of goods they are laying claim to. A debtor must then not sell these goods until the debt being claimed is paid. If the debt is not paid within a few days the bailiffs can return and collect the goods. Some bailiffs are kind and courteous – others are rough and aggressive. Stay calm when faced with a bailiff and just ensure they do not remove anything of importance without confirming their authority. Ring the police if things get out of hand.

Mainly use common sense. Our view is, if an individual is attempting to fend off visits by bailiffs, then that individual has allowed matters to get out of hand. The real problem needs to be addressed and resolved, rather than time being spent on worrying about what a bailiff can or cannot do. If an individual is under constant threats from bailiffs then it is generally time that that individual submitted to bankruptcy in order to gain protection from his creditors and to allow the resumption of normal living.

Charging Orders

A charging order can be made on a property at the discretion of a court when a creditor has a court judgement for a debt which has not been paid. If a court agrees, a charge can be placed on a property to secure the debt of an unpaid creditor who has an unpaid judgement debt. There are different kinds of charges that can be made. One type allows the charge-holder to force the sale of a property to recover his debt. Another type prevents the sale of the property but gives the charge-holder first claim on any surplus money when a property is sold. Someone with a charge or charges on their property should investigate their precise nature. If a creditor takes steps to obtain a charge against a debtor's property, then that debtor may seek the protection of bankruptcy to put a stop to such action. Once a bankruptcy order has been made creditors cannot then place charges on the bankrupt's property.

Child Support Agency

The Child Support Agency – known as the CSA – can order absent parents to make payments to the parent caring for their child or children. Enforcement of such orders is very tough. An earnings deduction order can be made and the CSA can send in bailiffs to seize goods if a liability order is made. There is currently no escaping claims made by the CSA. Even if the individual goes into bankruptcy, their claims must still be met. The position with the CSA is politically very volatile. The media have been active in the past publicising particularly bad hardship cases. As we write a new Labour government has recently been elected and it is quite possible they may change the CSA rules.

Citizens Advice Bureaux

Nearly every town in Britain has a Citizens Advice Bureau.

These are local charities operating under the umbrella of a national charity of Citizens Advice Bureaux. Their purpose is to provide free advice on any subject. Most of their enquiries concern benefit claims and debt problems. Because of their loose structure the quality of particular CABs – as they are known – varies enormously. Some have full time trained debt advisers, others operate using part-time volunteers. Their intervention with creditors can be helpful, particularly if someone is looking for more time to pay a debt or debts, when most bureaux will be happy to write to creditors on behalf of their clients to make them aware of the debtor's requirements.

Council Tax

Council tax should always be paid as a priority (see priority debts below). Failing to pay council tax debts can ultimately lead to imprisonment.

Court Fines

As with council tax the failure to pay court fines can also lead to imprisonment so they, too, should be paid as a matter of priority. Even if a person goes bankrupt they must still pay any fines imposed by a court.

Credit Agreements

Goods bought on a credit sale are owned immediately by the consumer (unlike hire purchase – see below). The creditor loaning the money can chase the buyer for the money owed but they cannot seize back the goods in the case of default on that particular agreement.

Credit Rating

Once a person starts failing to pay debts as they are due, their credit rating will rapidly become damaged. Most creditors these days run credit checks through various credit rating agencies before they will allow someone credit. These agencies are constantly collecting information on individuals. Court judgements against people will be instantly picked up. Once the credit rating of a person living at a particular address is damaged, it may also effect anyone else living at the same address eg a spouse or children. This will make it very difficult for people at the affected address to obtain credit.

Hire Purchase

A hire purchase agreement hires goods to a person for a particular period. This type of agreement these days is most commonly used for the purchase of motor vehicles. If a person defaults on a hire purchase agreement then, depending on how much has been paid, the hirer may be able to recover the particular item if they obtain a court order, or without a court order if only a small amount has been paid. In other words, if someone buys a car on hire purchase, and immediately defaults on payments, the hirer has the right to recover the car.

Joint Debts

If there are joint debts, eg husband and wife have a joint mortgage and one of them either fails to pay their share of their debt, or goes into bankruptcy, then the other person involved then becomes liable for the entire debt. People very commonly think that if they have a joint debt with someone else they are only liable for half of the debt. This is not the case. Any creditor can chase either person involved in a joint debt for full amount of the money owed.

Maintenance

From April 1993 child maintenance powers passed to the Child Support Agency (see above) but arrears due under existing court orders still exist. Failure to pay maintenance can lead to imprisonment so it should be treated as a priority debt (see priority debts below).

Mortgage Arrears

If people fail to pay their mortgages and arrears build up on their mortgage account, then eventually the lender will move to repossess the property involved. Usually a court will give possession to the mortgage lender unless the borrower can demonstrate that they can pay off, or at least substantially reduce, the arrears within a short time or, in certain circumstances, if they can demonstrate to the court that they could pay of the outstanding debt over the remaining period of the mortgage. Once a creditor obtains legal possession over a property it can then apply to the court to have the people occupying it evicted. Mortgage arrears should therefore be taken very seriously indeed. Either a first mortgage holder or a second mortgage holder can take this action.

Mortgage Shortfalls

When a house is repossessed by a lender, it will eventually be sold, either by private treaty or by auction. If the money raised from the sale is not enough to repay the mortgage, then the amount of money left owing is known as a shortfall. Often the shortfall does not arise for some considerable time after the property is repossessed. Some people who have had their homes repossessed are surprised and upset when, perhaps a few years after repossession, they receive letters demanding that mortgage shortfalls of thousands of pounds be repaid. Banks and building societies pursue these shortfalls with considerable vigour. Anyone who has had their home repossessed needs to be aware of this. An individual who has had his home repossessed should not attempt to purchase another property until any possible shortfall created upon the sale of the first property has been addressed.

Priority Debts

Certain debts are known to debt advisers as priority debts. Priority debts should be paid first. Thus any debts which may lead to imprisonment, such as court fines, council tax and maintenance orders, should be paid first. The next priority are debts which may lead to the loss of a home. These may be mortgage repayments or rent. The final priority debts are the major utilities ie gas, electricity and water. Failing to pay utility bills will lead to these supplies eventually being cut off. Next in line are any hire purchase debts. If these payments are not maintained, then the lender may be able to quickly seize these goods. Some people may have some slightly different priority debts. A student, for example, may need to pay a course fee to further his education. In such a case the course fee would be a priority debt. It is simple common sense to give these particular debts priority, but it is amazing how many people pay off less important debts first, perhaps because they have come under pressure from threatening phone calls or letters. An unsecured credit card lender, for example, cannot injure a debtor in the short term in the way that a gas or electric company can.

Debts other than priority debts should be paid only if there is money to spare after the priority debts have been paid. Unfortunately some of the less scrupulous lenders, be they banks, building societies or credit card companies often adopt intimidatory tactics such as telephoning the debtor early on a morning, constantly during the day and throughout the evening, or writing letters on a daily basis. These actions often encourage a debtor, out of fear, to make payments to them and therefore leave themselves unable to pay priority debts.

Remittance of Debts

Certain bodies have the power to remit (or forgive) certain debts. The Magistrate Courts have the power to remit fines or council tax arrears in cases of severe hardship. The local authority may write off rates owed in certain cases. The Inland Revenue also has the power to forgive debts. It must be emphasised here that this is only done in cases of severe hardship and the most likely candidates would be non-property owners on unemployment or social security benefits. Property owners would be most unlikely to be forgiven any debts.

Rent Arrears

As with mortgage arrears, failure to pay rent on a property will eventually lead to the person involved being evicted by the landlord.

Standing Guarantor

Someone who signs a form guaranteeing someone else's debt becomes liable for that debt in full, if the original borrower fails to honour his agreement. The person who has guaranteed the debt can be pursued as if they were the person who borrowed the money in the first place.

Time Orders

Time orders have been the subject of considerable controversy in recent years. They are theoretically a method of applying to a court for more time to pay certain debts. Until the legal controversy surrounding the application of such orders has been cleared up, we cannot recommend their use in a general sense, and see little point in discussing them here.

CHAPTER 3

THE BUSINESS DEBTOR

By the term 'business debtor' we mean anyone in debt who is running a business. Three million people in Britain run their own businesses. They face a special set of problems and different types of complicated side issues. As with consumer debtors, a business in debt is faced with the same four basic choices, although the manner of dealing with them may be different: These choices are:

1) REPAY DEBTS IN FULL
2) REPAY DEBTS IN PART
3) GO BANKRUPT
4) RUN AWAY

REPAY DEBTS IN FULL

Turn the Business Around

It is sometimes possible to turn around the fortunes of an ailing business by working harder, because good health has been recovered after an illness, or simply because there has been a recent upturn in trade. In our experience, however, many entrepreneurs are overly optimistic in this respect. For instance, they sometimes relate the size of their turnover to their debt burdens. They might be running a Spar shop, for example, with a turnover of £350,000 and on that basis believe they can service debts of £100,000. The fact that they fail to address is that profit margins can be so low and that they might only be achieving £35,000 by way of net profit.

If there is a family to support there will be very little left to service debts once the taxman has had his cut. We are constantly surprised how many people running their own business look at the turnover of that business, as opposed to the profit margins. People in business need to be realistic about their future prospects. There is little point in continuing to put effort into running a business overburdened by debt. No matter what the turnover of that business is, if the profit margins are not high enough to cover the overheads, nothing will be achieved.

By definition, an entrepreneur is likely to have an optimistic nature and will be much more likely to take a risk than a person in paid, relatively secure employment, such as a civil servant or policeman. Equally, because of that more optimistic nature, they are often more unwilling to face reality.

Cease Trading and Sell Up

Sometimes it will be possible, with a business that is losing money, to cease trading in order to cap the losses and prevent further debts from building up. Any property and/or other assets may then be sold to pay off creditors in full. If a business continues to trade when it is losing money, it becomes less and less likely, as each day passes, that such an action will succeed.

Sell the Business as a Going Concern

If a business can be sold as a going concern, it is often worth up to 50 per cent more than the bricks and mortar value. Further funds are likely to be raised by selling the stock at its valuation figure. In our experience, however, especially as we write this book and, indeed, over the last few years, it is extremely difficult to sell any business as a going concern, never mind one that is clearly losing money. Small independent retailers, no matter what their trade, be it a newsagent, china store, butcher or whatever have all been affected badly by the change in trading patterns over recent years. Large supermarkets now sell a much wider variety of goods, often at more competitive prices. This has affected the turnover of most small shopkeepers.

Nothing is impossible, however, and this course of action should at least be explored.

Negotiate with Creditors

If a business has ceased to trade or has been sold and debts from that business still exist, it may be possible to negotiate with the creditors of that business. If the former owner, for instance, is fortunate enough to locate employment, he may be able to make funds available from his earnings to make weekly or monthly payments to reduce his indebtedness. He may also have personal assets which he is able to sell, given time. Many creditors, rather than seeing the individual go into bankruptcy, will exercise patience if kept fully informed of the actions being taken and/or receive regular payments on their accounts. As a general rule, if creditors are treated properly, they, in turn, will behave properly or at least be more reasonable.

REPAY DEBTS IN PART

Negotiate with Creditors

The simplest, least expensive and, our wide experience, most effective way of coming to an arrangement with creditors is by direct negotiation. Debtors with good communication skills may attempt to reach agreement with creditors whereby they repay a percentage of their debts in full settlement. Solicitors, accountants, CABs and other money advice agencies will sometimes carry out these negotiations for debtors, with varying degrees of skill and success.

A major problem facing many debtors is the inadequacy of the advice offered by solicitors, accountants and other advisers, as well as their own lack of administrative skills.

The Bankruptcy Association was founded initially as a specialist agency to provide competent and effective advice. We now carry out hundreds of negotiations with creditors each year, reaching agreements to avoid the necessity of bankruptcy. Many agreements have been reached with creditors whereby they have accepted a few pence in the pound, in full settlement of particular debts. There are technical difficulties in ensuring that informal arrangements are legally binding. These can, however, be overcome if the matter is approached in the proper manner, by a competent, caring and skilled negotiator.

Of course, it is not always possible to negotiate a settlement, sometimes a single creditor owed a relatively small amount may refuse an agreement made with the other, larger, creditors. Nonetheless successful conclusions are reached in a large percentage of the cases we handle.

It is possible to set up these informal arrangements in every country of the United Kingdom.

Individual Voluntary Arrangement

It is now possible for individual debtors to enter into a formal voluntary arrangement known as an IVA (individual voluntary arrangement). These arrangements are legal contracts for the satisfaction of debts, either in whole or in part, and such arrangements, if voted in, are binding on all unsecured creditors, subject to limited technical exceptions which may cause difficulties.

We were very keen on these arrangements when they first became available in 1987 and encouraged hundreds of people to take this route. However, bitter experience of watching them fail, time after time, often because of excessive demands made by creditors, and inadequate or incorrect advice given by so-called professional advisers, have left us very wary of recommending this course of action.

A voluntary arrangement is an offer made to unsecured creditors, by an individual in financial trouble, to perhaps dispose of assets and/or make a contribution from future earnings, to pay out a dividend to those unsecured creditors in full settlement of their debts. Secured creditors may also be bound by the arrangement as long as they have been given notice of their entitlement to vote. A proposal must be made to, and through, an insolvency practitioner, who is a person specifically authorised to deal with such matters. Insolvency practitioners are usually qualified as either accountants or solicitors. In practice, they help prepare the proposal and should act as an independent intermediary between the debtor and the creditors, thereby ensuring that the proposal is realistic and represents a fair balance between the interests of all concerned. Once a proposal has been prepared, an application is made to the court for an Interim Order. This protects the debtor from further legal action by creditors. That protection prevents the issue of a bankruptcy petition or the hearing of a petition which has already been issued. The purpose is to maintain the current position until the creditors have had the opportunity to consider the proposal, at a meeting called by the insolvency practitioner for that purpose. Such a meeting will be called, unless the insolvency practitioner reports to the court that there is no reasonable prospect of reaching an agreement with the creditors.

Arrangements may involve the disposal of assets, so that the proceeds may be shared amongst the creditors. Payments may be made by the debtor from future income or from trading receipts. Sometimes funds may be made available by a friend or relative, in return for creditors accepting the proposal. Any combination is possible. Often the debtor will wish to keep his home, in return for payments from his future earnings or from a third party.

All creditors may vote on the proposal, either by being present in person, by sending a representative or by sending a postal vote. The votes of secured creditors only count to the extent that their security is insufficient to cover their lending. Voting power is according to money owed to individual creditors. It then requires the agreement of 75 per cent, by money value, of those creditors who trouble to vote, and whose votes are valid, to turn the proposal into a binding voluntary arrangement. This is subject to the proviso that there are at least 50 per cent in favour, ignoring the votes of connected persons, ie 'close relatives.'

If a voluntary arrangement succeeds, then bankruptcy is avoided. In law, individuals may then incur further credit. In reality, this is often found to be impossible as their credit rating is ruined because voluntary arrangements are recorded by credit reference agencies.

The costs of setting up the voluntary arrangement and supervising the implementation of it, if approved, should come from the monies which the arrangement provides to be distributed to creditors. In reality, however, most insolvency practitioners will be unwilling to act unless some, if not all, of the initial costs are paid to them in advance. This is because, if the arrangement is not approved, there will be no funds to cover their fees. Depending on the complexity of the case and the area in which the debtor resides, these costs can range between £1,000 and £5,000.

Anyone entering into a voluntary arrangement must adhere strictly to the agreed terms, otherwise the insolvency practitioner supervising the arrangement has little choice but to apply for the bankruptcy of the person involved. A good arrangement should allow some flexibility in the event of unforeseen circumstances. When arrangements do fail mid-term, the misery of the debt problem has simply been extended and because there are bankruptcy costs as well as the costs of the arrangement which went before, creditors also suffer a detriment.

It should also be pointed out that even if a bankruptcy order has been made against an individual, then a voluntary arrangement may still be attempted. If successful, it will have the effect of lifting the bankruptcy order.

There are many sharks in the insolvency world, some advertise in national newspapers, claiming to be able to save people from bankruptcy. These sharks often simply refer people to insolvency practitioners, collecting a fat fee for themselves, en route. From their own selfish point of view, it is in their interest to encourage people to go for voluntary arrangements, when this may not be the best option for the debtor. Those who are in financial difficulty should ensure that they contact someone appropriately experienced to give them guidance, such as the Bankruptcy Association.

To sum up, individual voluntary arrangements should be approached with extreme caution and they should only be considered if there is some real, practical benefit to the person involved. The mere avoidance of bankruptcy itself is not, in our view, sufficient justification for entering into such an arrangement.

This procedure is available to people resident in Northern Ireland as well as England and Wales, but is not available in Scotland.

Deeds of Arrangement

These were the predecessors to the more modern voluntary arrangements and for some curious reason were carried forward from old bankruptcy law into the Insolvency Act 1986. Only a handful are registered each year and they are, for all practical purposes, extinct. Anyone curious about these rarely used procedures should refer to a more detailed textbook.

GO BANKRUPT

If it is impossible to reach agreement with creditors over the repayment of debts and the debt problems are overwhelming, then it may well prove necessary to go into personal bankruptcy. This issue is discussed in the following chapter on bankruptcy.

RUN AWAY

Businesses can, and indeed do, often fail very quickly and dramatically. Sometimes within a few short months of starting a business an entrepreneur may have lost all his initial cash investment and be heavily in debt. To some people, understandably, the sudden shock to their system of finding their lives turned around so badly leads them to fall apart and run away from the problem. We know of many examples where people have simply fled the country, never mind their locality, due to the trauma of business failure. This, however, is a very unwise course of action.

A person who runs away from his creditors can be bankrupted in his absence. Any creditor owed £750 or more can apply to have a debtor bankrupted. If someone who runs away is bankrupted then that person may well be held in bankruptcy until such time as they reappear. This means that if the person who runs away subsequently rebuilds his life and perhaps buys property, then all this will be lost if, or when, they are discovered later. We have known several people to whom this has happened.

In other words, for a person to adopt this cause of action means that person must spend the rest of his life with a 'Sword of Damocles' hanging over his head. If a person is under such financial pressure that he feels like running away, then it makes much more sense to at least go bankrupt first. He will at least then get discharged from the bankruptcy after a few years and be able to breathe easily again. So if any reader is considering running away, we strongly advise against it for the reasons given above.

OTHER IMPORTANT ISSUES

Laid out below, in alphabetical order, we discuss a number of other common issues that effect people in business.

Bailiffs

Bailiffs are people who act on behalf of creditors, or the courts, to collect debts, seize goods or to repossess homes. There are many types of bailiffs, all with varying powers. Many people ask us each year about the rights and powers of bailiffs. Their powers vary according to the debt they are attempting to collect and, without a textbook on the complexities of bailiffs powers imprinted in our minds, it is generally impossible to say. In any event, many bailiffs themselves are unaware of their precise powers. Common sense needs to be applied when someone turns up on the doorstep with a court order claiming to be a bailiff.

If bailiffs arrive to repossess a home they have the power to physically remove people from a repossessed home and seize the property. If they arrive to collect unpaid debts they generally have the power to seize goods belonging to the debtor. In most cases they cannot seize personal belongings, bedding or items of household furniture necessary for everyday living. If they try to seize such intimate possessions they should be physically prevented until confirmation of the terms of any court order is precisely investigated and confirmed. They can often also take 'walking possession' of goods. This means that they make a list of goods they are laying claim to. A debtor must then not sell these goods until the debt being claimed is paid. If the debt is not paid within a few days the bailiffs can return to collect the goods. Some bailiffs are kind and courteous – others are rough and aggressive. Stay calm when faced with a bailiff and just ensure they do not remove anything of importance without confirming their authority. Ring the police if things get out of hand.

Mainly use common sense. Our view is, if an individual is attempting to fend off visits by bailiffs, then that individual has allowed matters to get out of hand. The real problem needs to be addressed and resolved, rather than time being spent on worrying about what a bailiff can or cannot do. If an individual is under constant threats from bailiffs then it is generally time that that individual submitted to bankruptcy in order to gain protection from his creditors and to allow the resumption of normal living.

Bankruptcy Neurosis

Some people suffer from a complete breakdown of normal judgement when they find themselves heading towards a bankruptcy scenario. This is particularly common in business because of the speed with which business debts can quickly build up. This was long ago labelled 'bankruptcy neurosis.' During the course of our work with the Bankruptcy Association we have also come across what we have called 'bankruptcy illness.' Some people literally become physically ill as a direct result of money worry. More extreme cases end up in mental hospitals. This failure to face up to reality invariably exacerbates the problems that have to be faced at the end of the day. Other people have an absolute horror of the prospect of bankruptcy. These problems mainly affect men, although a small number of women have the same reactions. Any reader of this book feeling this way should understand it is not uncommon, and every person in serious debt will have these kinds of feelings, to some degree. It is important to try and set aside such emotional feelings when deciding how to deal with debt problems. Money is a very black and white thing. Creditors are owed it and they want it. If a debtor cannot pay he must come up with a suitable solution.

Credit Rating

There are two main credit reference agencies, CCN and Equifax. Those agencies keep records of court orders made against individuals and businesses. When an application for any form of credit is made, the lender will, in nearly every case, approach one of these agencies to carry out a credit check on the borrower. If that person has a poor credit rating, has had problems in the past, has been or is bankrupt, for instance, then the chances are that the application will be refused. An individual may write to either of these agencies and request a copy of his credit file.

Debt Advisers

In recent years, debt has been seen by many people to be a 'growth industry' and debt advisers in various guises, have set up in business in profusion. A few offer a useful service. Equally, however, many are unauthorised, inexperienced and often incompetent. Great care should be taken by an individual seeking advice on debt problems. Sadly, much responsibility must be accepted by the debtor when approaching such people. We have great sympathy and understanding with people with serious financial problems and do understand that such people are often desperate for assistance and support. It constantly surprises us, however, how many people do not check out advisers and appear to be willing to hand over often considerable funds (usually in cash) when requested by unscrupulous, so called 'professionals'. If a person advertises through a box number in local or national newspapers, does not have an office, arranges to meet a debtor in the local pub or at the debtors home, beware. Equally, the debtor should think through the offers and/or promises these people often make. Many are, quite frankly, illegal and cannot be honoured.

Insolvency Practitioners

An insolvency practitioner is usually an accountant or a solicitor. He will be authorised to act as a trustee in bankruptcy, a supervisor of a voluntary arrangement and as a liquidator of a limited company. There are several authorising bodies and he will have to obey the rules of that body. An insolvency practitioner may operate as a sole practitioner or be an employee of a large firm. By far the greatest majority of insolvency practitioners are decent, honest professionals, often doing a relatively unpopular job. However, there are a small number who see it as their right to abuse the debtor and treat them very badly. Unfortunately, these few cause the remainder of their profession to have a very poor reputation. A working party has recently been formed to oversee the activities of these people. We have high hopes that, through the activities of that working party, the unscrupulous and badly behaved characters will be brought to book. Anyone having cause for complaint against an insolvency practitioner may, of course, make a formal complaint to their authorising body. From experience we know that this has very little effect, but is the correct course of action to be followed.

Lease Agreements

People put their name to a lease agreement, often with little, if any, knowledge of the commitment they are assuming. Even now, after so many people have been bankrupted due to lease agreements during this latest, long and severe recession, solicitors and accountants are still advising people going into business to obtain as long a lease as possible, 'for security'. It needs to be clearly understood by anyone signing a lease agreement that they are responsible for the payments on that lease until the end of its term. Failure to make those payments, for whatever reason, will usually result in bankruptcy. To explain, if a person enters into a lease for 21 years (this is a very common term) and the business fails after 7 years, then that person will be responsible for the rent for the next 14 years. Very serious consideration should be given before a long lease is taken on.

Landlords' Rights

Landlords generally have very strong powers over business premises. Non payment of a single month's rent may empower a landlord to enter those premises, seize any goods therein and change the locks. Readers in business need to be aware of their vulnerability on this point.

Limited Companies

Limited companies were designed to limit the liability of the person running the business. In recent years, however, some people have abused their position by setting up a limited company, running up debts and then putting the company into liquidation and walking away from the problem without any personal liability. This has, unfortunately, meant that many honest, hard-working people running limited companies have been called upon by creditors (be they trade suppliers or banks) to provide personal guarantees, thus negating the advantages of a limited company. See chapter 5 for a fuller description of methods of dealing with the debts of a limited company

Partnerships

Partnerships are most certainly the worst kind of trading style. Very often a sole trader, upon advice from his accountant, makes his wife a partner 'for tax purposes'. The advantages gained are far outweighed by the liability on the spouse. If or when that business fails, then the spouse, who may have had no involvement whatsoever with the running of the business, is liable for all the debts of the business, along with her husband. In a partnership, all the partners are liable for all the debts. It is often much more difficult for partners to negotiate part repayments with creditors than for a sole trader. This is because creditors can call on at least two people, and perhaps more, to repay the debts owing. Often too partners fall out when financial problems arise and they often work against each others interests as a result. Unless all the partners of a business get together with a unified approach towards their creditors they will stand little chance of reaching a sensible settlement. Partnership bankruptcies are dealt with in the next chapter which covers bankruptcy in more detail.

Personal Guarantees

Personal guarantees have been increasingly requested in recent years. This has been for the reasons described in the limited company section above and simply due to the varying economic climate. In very simply terms, a person providing goods or a service to a limited company often requests a personal guarantee as a further security for his investment. Basically, by signing a personal guarantee a person is negating the advantages of trading as a limited company and accepts responsibility for any resultant debt.

Priority Debts

It is not easy to advise on priority debts in a business situation. Different businesses may be vulnerable from different quarters. One business may need to pay off a trade creditor in order to get further supplies. Another may have the taxman about to arrive to seize goods that will put it out of business. Generally though, business rates and rents should have the highest priority for a business that is trading, as well as the general utilities bills.

Property as Security

It is very common for people in business to offer any property they might own as security for bank loans for example. Sometimes too, the spouse of the person in business may put up their share of any jointly owned property as security as well. It is important to understand that if the terms of the loan are not honoured, then in most cases the lenders will call in their security and move for possession and sale of the property involved. In rare cases, perhaps if the people involved are very old, then lenders might wait until they die. It is sadly not uncommon for parents of people in business to offer their own homes as security for business loans for their children. Again it should be understood that if things do not work out the lenders will force the sale of the parental home. Many borrowers seem to think that lenders will wait until they decide to sell their home before collecting on their security. This sometimes happens, but very rarely. More often, lenders move very quickly for possession and sale of any property that is securing a loan.

Tax and VAT Debts

The tax authorities can issue their own warrants to seize goods for outstanding debts. They do not need a court order. They usually send in private bailiffs accompanied by a tax officer to seize goods.

CHAPTER 4

BANKRUPTCY

When and Why to Go Bankrupt

Few people relish the prospect of going bankrupt. They see it as a humiliating process and, indeed, it is. Some have to be dragged through the process kicking and screaming. Others are glad of the relief from pursuing creditors that a bankruptcy order brings. These internalised personal feelings often mean that individual people in debt are their own worst advisers. People in financial trouble should try to set aside their internalised feelings (no easy matter) and look at their problems objectively.

Take the hypothetical case of Peter who has run a business which has failed. He has sold his home in an attempt to stave off business collapse, but in the end he has failed and has no assets left. Peter is now in rented accommodation, unemployed and with tens of thousands of pounds of debts which are causing him desperate worry.

In this example, Peter has, in effect, already suffered the worst effects of business failure, ie loss of his home and occupation. He now stands to gain some relief from a bankruptcy, although he may not relish the prospect. He will then be protected from his creditors. During the course of the bankruptcy, as long as he does not inherit or win money, or earn more than he needs to live to a reasonable standard, he will not be required to make any payments to his trustee in bankruptcy. Upon discharge he will be free to rebuild his life anew.

It is this kind of pragmatic reasoning which needs to be applied to people with financial problems. People in debt can be compared to the captain of a sinking ship. A prudent captain will do all he can to save his ship from sinking. It would be foolish if the ship were to go down with all hands, as a result of his efforts. At some point he must decide if the position is hopeless and then save his crew and himself and what possessions he can, by taking to the lifeboats. Bankruptcy may be, in many cases, the lifeboat which a person in debt must take to, after considering the alternatives discussed in the previous chapters.

The previous chapters describe the methods of avoiding bankruptcy. In many cases, however, it simply cannot be avoided, either because creditors are determined to bankrupt those who owe them money, or because debtors have found it impossible to reach agreement with creditors. In such instances bankruptcy will ensue.

There are three ways to go bankrupt. A creditor owed at least £750 can bring a petition against a person owing them that money, or a debtor can bring a petition against himself. A person involved in an individual voluntary arrangement can also be bankrupted by the supervisor of his arrangement, if he fails to comply with the terms of the arrangement. There are no restrictions on who can bankrupt themselves in England, Wales and Northern Ireland, although there are restrictions in Scotland.

Creditor's Petition

A creditor may bring a bankruptcy petition against anyone who owes him £750 or more (as at 1 July 1997), or two or more creditors may combine together, as long as the debts equal that amount. The normal procedure is that a creditor must first serve a statutory demand on the debtor, demanding payment of the debt within three weeks. If the debt is not paid within this time, then the creditor can proceed to issue a bankruptcy petition against the debtor. If someone disputes the debt claimed in the statutory demand, then an application may be made to have it set aside.

Debtor's Petition

A debtor can bring his own bankruptcy petition by obtaining a bankruptcy petition form from his local county court (or from the High Court in the Strand for those living within the London insolvency district). On completion of this form, which lists debts, assets and other information, a telephone call to the court should be made, to arrange an appointment for a bankruptcy hearing. The completed form is then taken to the court with the necessary fee in cash (this is £307 for an individual and £7 extra for each partnership, as at 1 July 1997). The current fee should be ascertained with the relevant court. A bankruptcy order will normally be made immediately, on the presentation of the fee and the petition. If it is vital that a bankruptcy order be made immediately and the local court for some reason is not available (some courts do not have a district judge available every weekday), then an order may be sought from an alternative court. Each local court should know which is the alternative court to be used.

In cases, however, where a debtor declares assets of at least £2,000 and debts of less than £20,000, then the court may not make a bankruptcy order, but may send the debtor to see an insolvency practitioner to ascertain if a voluntary arrangement would be an appropriate option. (It is quite beyond our understanding as to why this odd provision is part of our bankruptcy laws). Voluntary arrangements are explained in the previous chapters.

The Immediate Aftermath of a Bankruptcy Order

Once a bankruptcy order has been made, then all the assets and property of the bankrupt person (with certain exceptions explained later) vest in the trustee in bankruptcy, who initially is the official receiver, an employee of the Insolvency Service (an executive agency of the Department of Trade and Industry). There are around forty official receivers' offices in England and Wales, each with its own official receiver and supporting staff of examiners and others.

If a debtor has brought a bankruptcy petition against himself, then he usually speaks by telephone to his local official receiver from the court, after the bankruptcy order has been made. The official receiver will ask for details of the bankrupt's bank accounts and other information. He will normally arrange an appointment for the bankrupt to attend his office for an interview. Depending on the information given by the bankrupt to the official receiver, then he might arrange for agents to immediately visit the bankrupt's business address to seize assets. It is very unusual, however, for the official receiver to send anyone to the bankrupt's home address in England and Wales.

Any bank or building society accounts in which the bankrupt has an interest (including any joint accounts) will normally be frozen immediately by the official receiver. Thus a husband and wife with a joint account would have any funds in the account frozen, even if only one of them go bankrupt. The money belonging to the non-bankrupt spouse would be returned in due course, but this will take time and could cause great inconvenience and distress. For this and other reasons, it is important that the non-bankrupt spouse open their own separate account before the bankruptcy, in order to avoid these problems.

If a creditor has brought the petition, then the bankrupt will usually be contacted immediately by the official receiver either by telephone or letter. Again, if the official receiver has reason to believe that there are substantial assets in place on business premises, then he may send someone immediately to seize these goods.

This is a brief outline of events which take place immediately after the making of the bankruptcy order. The sequence of these events vary from area to area. In some areas the official receiver's office is close to the court and a debtor bringing his own petition might be sent around immediately to the official receiver's office. The main point to be understood is that very rapid moves are made to seize the assets and property of the bankrupt. Readers need to be aware of this fact.

Income Payments Orders

A bankrupt person is entitled to earn sufficient money to cover all reasonable living expenses. If there is a surplus income after these expenses are met then the bankrupt is expected to pay a portion of any surplus to his trustee in bankruptcy. If there is a dispute the trustee can apply to a court to make an income payments order. The court will decide how much a bankrupt must pay. If this amount is not paid, without good reason, imprisonment may follow.

Council Tax

If adult people are living together in a property and one goes bankrupt, then the other adult or adults are liable for the current council tax that may be outstanding, although the bankrupt person is not. The bankrupt, however, is liable for future council tax from the date of the bankruptcy.

The Matrimonial Home

All property of the bankrupt may be sold by the trustee in bankruptcy, including the home of the bankrupt, whether he owns it entirely or in part. The non bankrupt spouse of a bankrupt is often entitled to a half share of the value of the home, whether or not the house is in joint names (this does not apply in Scotland). In addition, there is a twelve month protection from the trustee in bankruptcy before he can force the sale of the home if the bankrupt's wife and/or children, or someone else, also reside there. The non-bankrupt spouse is currently given the opportunity to save the home by purchasing the beneficial interest of the bankrupt. (This position may change in the future). The trustee will require the value of the bankrupt's share, although he may make an allowance for the fact that he does not have to pay the costs of a sale in such cases. Thus the non-bankrupt spouse may have to raise slightly less than half of the equity in the property, to secure the home.

Pension Rights in Bankruptcy

Certain pension rights in bankruptcy may be seriously affected. A court ruling reported at the beginning of 1997 confirmed that a trustee is entitled to both the lump sum element of a pension and the income from it, in certain cases. Even after a person is discharged from bankruptcy this money may still be claimed. Most private pensions and some occupational pensions may be vulnerable to such attack. Anyone with a substantial pension fund contemplating bankruptcy should check the position regarding their own pension with their pension company or employers.

Exempt Property

Certain property is exempt from bankruptcy proceedings and it is worth quoting the precise letter of the law because, over the years, we have come across many instances whereby official receivers and trustees have overstepped the law and seized exempt property. The appropriate legal reference is section 283 of the the Insolvency Act 1986. This section states that all property of the bankrupt vests in the trustee except for:

'such tools, books, vehicles and other items of equipment as are necessary to the bankrupt for use personally by him in his employment, business or vocation.' (section 283 subsection 2(a))'

'such clothing, bedding, furniture, household equipment and provisions as are necessary for satisfying the basic domestic needs of the bankrupt and his family.' (section 283 subsection 2(b))'

The rule of thumb applied by the authorities is that they will allow a bankrupt to keep any particular item referred to above which is worth less than £500. Therefore a car worth more than £500 would be seized, as would a piece of antique furniture worth thousands of pounds. An ordinary person living in a typical semi-detached home with household equipment of normal value would be left with everything intact. Likewise a builder or photographer, or any one else running a business, should be left with all items of equipment and vehicles worth less than £500 each.

Partnership Bankruptcies

This section deals with partnership law as it effects the more typical partnerships comprising for example, of three brothers, a husband and wife team or three or four colleagues. The law for larger partnerships and/or those containing a corporate partner is more complex and is not covered here.

There is a common misconception that if there are three partners in a business partnership which owes £30,000, then each partner is liable for, and can only be pursued for, £10,000. This is not so. Each partner is liable for the entire partnership debt.

Creditors can pursue the entire partnership by having it wound up as a limited company and having the assets of the partnership sold. To complicate matters even further, they can then, at the same time, or later, pursue any or all of the partners into personal bankruptcy, in order to force the sale of their personal property, such as their family homes.

Creditors can also choose to obtain bankruptcy orders against individual partners without winding up the partnership as a whole!

The best way to illustrate the draconian nature of partnership insolvency is to use a typical case as an example.

Let us say a partnership with three partners runs into trouble, with debts of £400,000. The partnership jointly owns property worth £100,000 and each partner owns his own home, valued at £150,000. A creditor petitions to have the partnership wound up and a liquidator is appointed to dispose of all of the partnership assets. He would take his expenses and fees first, and then pay out a dividend to creditors.

Later on, creditors may petition to have each of the partners bankrupted. A trustee in bankruptcy would then be appointed in each case to dispose of the each partner's home.

The running order of this procedure could be random and arbitrary, at the whim of creditors. They could bankrupt one partner rather than another, or two of them, or all of them. Also, the creditors could choose to bankrupt just two of the three partners and sell their homes to clear the partnership debts. The two partners selected would have to bear the full consequences. If this occurred, then these two partners could pursue claims against the one remaining partner, in an attempt to recover some of their own losses.

A partnership can also bring a bankruptcy order against itself, but all of the partners must agree to this. If a partnership bankrupts itself, and if all of the partners agree, this can have the effect of bankrupting the partnership as a whole, as well as each partner individually. This is because a partnership has its own common debts, whereas each individual partner may have additional personal borrowing. Thus a partnership bankruptcy usually creates a series of bankruptcies. If any partner does not agree to the partnership being bankrupted as a whole, then any partner can bankrupt himself as an individual. He would then immediately cease to be a partner in the partnership and his trustee in bankruptcy would then look to the other partners for his share of any partnership assets.

It should be clear to readers from the above, and for many other reasons too complex to explain here, that business partnerships are potential nightmares when things go wrong. The law is very complex and usually has devastating effects on all of the partners.

Partnership law has similar effects in every country in the United Kingdom, although the above comments are based on the law in England and Wales.

Discharge From a First Bankruptcy

An automatic discharge from a first bankruptcy is normally granted after three years. The discharge would only be suspended if the bankrupt had not co-operated with the proceedings or had broken the bankruptcy laws. If an official receiver or a trustee wishes to suspend a discharge and keep someone in bankruptcy, then he must make an application to the court, before the automatic discharge is due. The bankrupt would be informed of this application and it would then be the decision of the court, on hearing the evidence, to make such order as it thinks fit.

If a bankrupt brought the bankruptcy petition against himself and, in addition, had debts of less than £20,000, he would receive an automatic discharge after two years. If, however, a creditor brought a bankruptcy petition against someone owing less than £20,000, then an automatic discharge would not be granted until three years had passed.

CHAPTER 5

LIMITED COMPANIES

This chapter deals briefly with the position regarding limited companies which run into financial problems, as distinct from individuals, sole traders or partnerships, excepting that partnerships in England and Wales can be wound up as if they were limited companies in certain circumstances. Except for very minor differences in procedures, the law is almost identical in England, Wales, Scotland and Northern Ireland in so far as the treatment of limited companies is concerned. Although this chapter is based on the law in England, it is generally applicable throughout the United Kingdom.

Directors of limited companies should remember that except when a company is forcibly wound up, or put into receivership, then the fees need to be found, and usually paid up front, to follow voluntary winding up procedures. These procedures can be expensive, often running into thousands of pounds.

The concept of limited liability is more than one hundred years old and was introduced to provide protection for those in business, at a time of rapid commercial expansion, during the nineteenth century. It was designed to remove some of the risks involved from individual businessmen and to spread that risk amongst creditors. The habit of banks, landlords and others, however, in seeking personal guarantees from directors has increasingly eroded the concept of limited liability. In addition, the Insolvency Act 1986 introduced 'wrongful trading' provisions. Directors, or even 'shadow' directors, of a company, who are believed to have acted irresponsibly may now be, and have been, made liable in whole, or in part, for the debts of a limited company.

There are currently six major methods to deal with insolvent companies. These are:

1) Company voluntary arrangements
2) Administration orders
3) Receivership
4) Members' voluntary winding up
5) Creditors' voluntary winding up
6) Winding up by the court

The legal term 'winding up' is invariably referred to, both inside and outside of the insolvency profession, as 'liquidation'. For the purposes of this chapter therefore, the terms liquidation and winding up have the same meaning.

Company Voluntary Arrangements

One method of dealing with insolvency is a company voluntary arrangement. A company director may apply for a voluntary arrangement for his company at anytime. A voluntary arrangement is a proposal put to creditors, to dispose of stock and assets and/or make a contribution from future earnings, to pay out a dividend to creditors, in full settlement of a company's debts. It requires the agreement of 75 per cent of unsecured creditors by money value, to accept such a proposal, which then becomes binding on all unsecured creditors.

In practice, these arrangements for limited companies are not working out very well, for a number of reasons. First, it is costly to set up an arrangement for a company (several thousand pounds in most cases). Secondly, a company's creditor and debtor position is usually rapidly changing and it is difficult to forecast future cashflow. Thirdly, banks who hold securities are usually keen to enforce those securities.

Administration Orders

The administration order procedure allows a company's directors, or its creditors, to apply to the Court to have an administrator take over the running of a company's affairs.

An administration order can best be described as a half-way house between solvency and receivership. The idea behind the appointment of an administrator is that he has wider and more flexible powers to run a company as a going concern, than a receiver. He will, hopefully, be able to pull the company through its difficulties.

In practice, many administration orders have merely been the means of realising assets, before formal liquidation has taken place. In a few special cases, such as football clubs, administration orders have worked well. In many other cases, however, they have proved an unnecessary and expensive formality. They have not generally proved very practical.

Receivership

The various types of receivership are too complex to outline in detail. Suffice it to say that the appointment of a receiver is generally at the instigation of a major creditor (more often than not the bank). Quite often a bank will have an automatic power to appoint a receiver, even without applying to the court, if they follow specified procedures. By such methods the control of businesses can be torn from the control of their directors, and sold off, sometimes within hours, to their competitors. There are grave concerns about these procedures.

Receivership usually signals the quick and sudden death knell for a company, resulting fairly quickly in the closing of its operations, the dismissal of all staff, and the rapid sale and disposal of the company or its assets.

Members' Voluntary Winding Up

A members liquidation can take place when, although a company is unable to pay its debts on time, it can do so within a period of twelve months.

The directors swear out a 'statutory declaration of solvency' and the shareholders may then appoint their own liquidator to deal with the company's affairs.

Creditors' Voluntary Winding Up

In a creditors' voluntary liquidation, the shareholders pass a resolution for the winding up of a company and then appoint a liquidator of their choice, to be the liquidator of the company. A meeting of the company's creditors then takes place, who may approve of the appointed liquidator, or alternatively, appoint one of their own choice.

Winding Up by the Court

Any creditor of a company with an overdue debt of £750, or a combination of creditors owed that amount or more, may issue a formal demand for repayment. This may simply be by letter. On the basis of that demand, an application may be made to have the company put into liquidation, if the debt has not been paid within three weeks. There is no need to have an unsatisfied judgement debt, before such a petition may be issued.

This leaves companies very exposed to their unsecured creditors, who can quickly and easily bring a company's operations to a halt.

When a company is wound up in this way, by order of the court, then the official receiver is automatically appointed liquidator. Later, if the company has sufficient assets, the official receiver will hold a meeting of creditors to appoint an insolvency practitioner to take over as liquidator.

Directors of companies wound up by the Court will face personal examination by the official receiver about the causes of the business failure. Winding up by the Court is, therefore, generally seen as the most serious form of liquidation, because of the implication that the directors may have acted irresponsibly, by not implementing an alternative procedure, before the creditors moved to wind up the company.

Other Points

Whichever of these routes is taken by a company in trouble, the receiver or liquidator is obliged to report on the conduct of the directors of the company to the Department of Trade and Industry. The DTI may use these reports to bring prosecutions under the Company Directors Disqualification Act 1986. This enables the court to disqualify irresponsible directors from taking part in the future management of another business, for prescribed periods.

A register of disqualifications is maintained from which information is obtained by credit reference agencies, who, in turn, transmit this information to their users.

Finally, directors of insolvent limited companies sometimes find themselves personally liable for borrowings from the company, such as director loan accounts, and certain tax debts. Directors of limited companies in trouble should make sure they take care not to get trapped in this way, by taking the appropriate advice.

CHAPTER 6

IMPORTANT FINAL WORDS

Having read our book through to this point, the reader will probably realise that there are few hard and fast rules for dealing with debt problems.

This book has been designed to give 'global' advice. We have purposefully avoided explaining the intricacies of various legal actions and attempted to help those suffering the trauma of debt problems in a more general fashion.

We speak to hundreds of people every month who are living with serious debt problems, attempting to handle negotiations with creditors, dealing with the actions of bailiffs and trying to avoid bankruptcy. Many become involved and weighed down with various incidental side issues which often result in the real problem not being addressed as well or as promptly as necessary. Whilst we have great understanding and sympathy for anyone struggling with debt, we often find that their financial position is made worse by their failure (or indeed, the failure of their professional advisers) to address the root of the problem.

In very simple terms there are, as we have said in previous chapters, only four ways to resolve debt problems, namely: pay in full, negotiate a reduced payment in full and final settlement with the creditors, go into bankruptcy or run away. We have never met, in the 14 year history of the Bankruptcy Association, anyone who has succeeded in the last option.

Advising on debt problems can be, and often is, very complicated. Even if the actual course to be followed is clear cut, very often the debtors themselves bring with them their own views, fears and wishes. Circumstances often arise where it is patently obvious the debtor is unable to service his debts in any shape or form. However, that person may hold the view that to go into bankruptcy is dishonourable and to be avoided at all costs. Such a person needs to be lead gently through his problems until his fears and doubts are overcome. This is in the best interest not only of the debtor, but also to the benefit of the creditors. The longer a problem is allowed to go on, the less patience is shown by creditors. Some people may see our way of thinking and advising as brutal. It is not. It is simply realistic. Problems do not go away of their own accord. They must be handled properly for the benefit of all concerned.

There is little point in a debtor with no assets and little disposable income agreeing to make weekly or monthly repayments which he knows, in his heart, he will be unable to maintain, unless he is absolutely certain that his financial position will improve, allowing him to resolve his problem. Unfortunately, in the current economic climate, few, if any people, can have that certainty. To agree to repayment proposals which cannot be adhered to simply extends the agony for the debtor and tests the patience of the creditors.

Having said that, unless the debt is obviously of such proportions set against the assets and income of the debtor that it is patently impossible to make a realistic proposal, then it is always worth approaching creditors with some offer of repayment in an effort to avoid bankruptcy.

As advisers with vast negotiating experience, it is difficult, if not impossible, even for us to give an indication of how successful negotiations are likely to be. Not only should the size of the offer be considered, but consideration needs to be given to the number of creditors, who those creditors are (government departments, lending institutions, trade or personal creditors, etc), the past history of the debtor and the attitude of the lender all need to be taken into consideration.

We have dealt with many negotiations whereby the debtor has had perhaps 8 or 10 creditors and we have been able to reach agreement with them all, giving, in effect, our negotiating service 100 per cent success. Equally, there are creditors who are completely intransigent and a person having a single debt to just one of that type of creditor has no chance of reaching agreement. One of the main features and functions of the Bankruptcy Association, aside from giving help and advice on bankruptcy, serious debt and related issues, is to negotiate with creditors. Within the negotiating service available to all Association members, we have brought thousands of cases to a successful conclusion, helping hundreds of people avoid bankruptcy, at the same time giving a return to creditors which they would not have received if the debtor had taken that route.

As we write this book, we have reached agreement with one bank owed around £20,000 on a payment of £500 in full and final settlement. That represents less than 3 per cent of the total debt. A building society has just accepted £1,000 against a liability of £80,000. That represents just over 1 per cent of the total debt. These two agreements alone have meant that two debtors have avoided the trauma of bankruptcy and given some return, albeit small, to the two creditors.

Hopefully, the above adequately confirms our statement that advising on debt problems is often complicated. Many factors need to be taken into consideration. We would also maintain that negotiations are better handled by an independent adviser, ie one who does not gain financially by the advice given to the debtor, or by the agreement reached.

Many people, suffering the stress and trauma of dealing with debt problems make proposals which they would not consider, if they were not in such a vulnerable position. We fully understand that someone being faced with losing their home or having the contents of their house seized by bailiffs acting for creditors will do almost anything in their power to avoid these consequences. We take dozens of calls from people wanting to know, for instance, what rights are held by bailiffs or how long a creditor will pursue a debt. Whilst we are happy to supply answers to such questions, we always qualify our response by explaining that, if that is the position, then the root of the problem should be acknowledged and resolved, as opposed to time and effort being given to stave off what is very often in such circumstances, the inevitable outcome.

In short, many people, quite understandably, avoid dealing with the problem properly. This often results in increasing the pressure brought to bear upon them and simply compounds their problems.

We, having run the Bankruptcy Association for nearly 15 years, are fully aware of, and have every sympathy with, those struggling with debt problems. We hope that this 'global' guide will help and comfort such people. We acknowledge, however, that some people will require more detailed advice and support. That is available to all members of The Bankruptcy Association. Anyway wishing to take advantage of membership is most welcome to discuss their own personal financial position with the authors of this book. The Bankruptcy Association telephone number is: 01524 64305.